COPYCAT COOKBOOK
MADE SIMPLE

A Step By Step Cookbook to Prepare

Recipes from your Favorite Restaurants.

Coockery School

Table Of Contents

Introduction

Copycat Recipes are meals that are exactly the same as recipes you find on popular cooking websites or your favorite restaurants. We prepare this so that you can relish tasty, but hard to cook, food without spending hours in front of your stove. Our book is full of delicious Copycat Recipes that taste like the real thing while taking very little effort on your part.

A lot of people visit cooking sites because they're interested in trying a new recipe. Some people love the recipes but don't have hours to spend making them. It can be daunting to try a new recipe, especially if it's been made by an acclaimed chef. With Copycat Recipes you don't have to worry about agonizing over the measurements and details. You can simply enjoy your meal without worrying about spending too much time in the kitchen.

The benefit of Copycat Recipes is that you can enjoy a delicious meal without having to spend hours in the kitchen. It's even easier since these recipes come from some of the most popular restaurants around the country. They use things you've likely already got in your kitchen, and they only take little effort to make.

There are many wonderful food websites out there with excellent recipes for all kinds of food. However, most of these sites don't provide ingredient lists or measurements for their recipes. For someone that's new to cooking this can be very frustrating. Even seasoned chefs have trouble following recipes that don't have details about how much sugar or butter goes into them.

The Importance of Copycat Recipes

Copycat recipes are important for several reasons:

1. They provide us the chance to make our favorite dishes quickly and easily. Preparing complicated dishes is often not possible because we don't have enough time. Copycat Recipes can provide us with the same taste we crave but in a more convenient format.

2. Such recipes can help us discover new dishes. Even if we have an idea of what we want to cook, it can be hard to come up with something exceptional and fascinating. Copycat Recipes are a good starting point for anyone who wants to make something new and exciting.

3. Such recipes can reduce our reliance on restaurant meals. Instead of calling the waiter over and spending a lot of money, we can make a tasty meal at home for far less money. We also don't have to wait for someone to bring us our food.

4. When we cook at home, we can use healthier ingredients and control the overall amount of fat, sugar, salt and other ingredients in our meal. Cooking your own food is the only way you can make sure it's exactly what you want it to be.

5. Copycat Recipes are more likely to taste as good as the original dishes because they are made by people who actually try out their recipes instead of finding a random recipe online and giving it a shot.

6. Copycat recipes are a great way to preserve the tastes of your favorite restaurants. Every time you visit a restaurant, it's possible that they'll change the menu or even close down. Now you can always be able to enjoy the food of your favorite restaurants with Copycat Recipes.

Copycat Recipes are very important because they help people save time and money. The main reason why people prepare food is that they want to eat it, of course. People also eat food to please their loved ones or friends or even employees in the case of restaurants.

Origin of Copycat Recipes

The concept of Copycat Recipes dates back to the Ancient Roman Empire. In Rome, there was a man who called himself Marcus Apicius. He was not just a chef but also an author who hosted a show about cooking. Marcus Apicius's recipes were very popular because they were delicious and original.

Copycat Recipes did not become widespread until the 1300s when French chefs started creating recipes that mimicked those of noblemen and kings. Later, the term became popular in restaurants in New York City around the 1920s and people started using it to refer to simple dishes made from available ingredients at home.

Today many people use Copycat Recipes because they're formulated by people who know what they are doing. They are made by people who know what the best flavor combinations are and how to make food that is packed with nutrients, yet still delicious.

Copycat Recipes often come from top-rated restaurants and don't just provide a recipe. They will also give you guidelines on how to make your meal as good as it can be.

Breakfast, Brunch and Appetizers Recipes

McDonald's Sausage Egg McMuffin

Preparation Time: 10 minutes
Cooking Time: 15 minutes
Servings: 4

Ingredients:

- 4 English muffins, cut in half horizontally
- 4 slices American processed cheese
- 1/2 tablespoon oil
- 1-pound ground pork, minced
- 1/2 teaspoon dried sage, ground
- 1/2 teaspoon dried thyme
- 1 teaspoon onion powder
- 3/4 teaspoon black pepper
- 3/4 teaspoon salt
- 1/2 teaspoon white sugar
- 4 large 1/3 -inch onion ring slices
- 4 large eggs
- 2 tablespoons water

Directions:

1. Preheat oven to 300°F.
2. Cover one half of muffin with cheese, leaving one half uncovered. Transfer both halves to a baking tray. Place in oven.
3. For the sausage patties, use your hands to mix pork, sage, thyme, onion powder, pepper, salt, and sugar in a bowl. Form into 4 patties. Make sure they are slightly larger than the muffins.

4. Heat oil in a pan. Cook patties on both sides for at least 2 minutes each or until all sides turn brown. Remove tray of muffins from oven. Place cooked sausage patties on top of the cheese on muffins. Return tray to the oven.
5. In the same pan, position onion rings flat into a single layer. Crack one egg inside each of the onion rings to make them round. Add water carefully into the sides of the pan and cover. Cook for 2 minutes.
6. Remove tray of muffins from the oven. Add eggs on top of patties, then top with the other muffin half.
7. Serve warm.

Nutrition:

Calories:453 Fat: 15 g Carbs: 67 g Protein: 15 g Sodium: 1008 mg

Jimmy Dean's Homemade Pork Sage Sausage

Preparation Time: 5 minutes
Cooking Time: 20 minutes
Servings: 4

Ingredients:

- 1-pound ground pork
- 1 teaspoon salt
- 1/2teaspoon dried parsley
- 1/4teaspoon rubbed sage
- 1/4teaspoon black pepper, ground
- 1/4teaspoon dried thyme
- 1/4teaspoon coriander
- 1/4teaspoon seasoned salt

Directions:

1. Mix all ingredients in a bowl.
2. Shape into patties. Then, cook in a pan on medium heat until meat is brown on both sides and cooked through.
3. Serve.

Nutrition:

Calories: 313 Fat: 24 g Carbs: 4 g Protein: 19 g Sodium: 646 mg

Ihop's Scrambled Egg

Preparation Time: 5 minutes

Cooking Time: 5 minutes

Servings: 1

Ingredients

- 1/4cup pancake mix
- 1–2 tablespoons of o butter
- 6 large eggs
- Salt and pepper, to taste

Directions

1. Thoroughly beat the pancake mix and, therefore, the eggs together until no lumps or clumps remain.

2. Butter a pan over medium heat.

3. When the pan is hot enough, pour the egg mixture in the middle of the pan.

4. Add the salt and pepper and let the mixture sit for a few minutes.

5. When the egg starts cooking, start pushing the sides of the mixture toward the center of the pan. Continue until the whole mixture is cooked.

6. Serve and luxuriate in.

Nutrition:

Calories 870, Total Fat 54g, Carbohydrates 9g,
Protein 69g, Sodium 34.9 mg

Ihop's Buttermilk Pancake

Preparation time: 5 minutes

Cooking time: 8 minutes

Servings: 8 to 10

Ingredients

- 11/4cups of all-purpose flour
- 1 teaspoon of baking soda
- 1 teaspoon of baking powder
- 11/4cups of granulated sugar
- 1 pinch salt
- 1 egg
- 11/4cups of buttermilk
- 1/4cup cooking oil

Directions

1. Preheat your pan by leaving it over medium heat while you're preparing the batter.
2. Take all of your dry ingredients and blend them.
3. Take all of your wet ingredients and blend them.
4. Carefully combine the dry mixture into the wet mixture until everything is mixed together entirely.
5. Melt some butter in your pan.
6. Slowly pour batter into the pan until you've got a 5-inch circle.
7. Flip the pancake when its edges seem to possess hardened.
8. Cook the opposite side of the hotcake also.
9. Repeat steps six through eight until your batter is finished.

10. Serve with softened butter and syrup.

Nutrition:

Calories 180.1, Total Fat 7.9g, Protein 4.1 g, Carbohydrates 23.2g
Sodium 271.6mg

Copycat Mozzarella Sticks

Preparation Time: 10 minutes
Cooking Time: 5 minutes
Servings: 16

Ingredients:

- 2/3 cup all-purpose flour
- 2 large eggs
- 1/4cup milk
- 1 cup Japanese breadcrumbs
- 1/2cup Parmesan cheese
- 1 tablespoon dried parsley
- 1/2teaspoon garlic salt
- 1/2teaspoon seasoning salt
- 8 pieces' mozzarella string cheese
- 1-quart vegetable oil
- Marinara sauce

Directions:

1. Add flour to a bowl. Then, in a separate bowl, mix eggs and milk. Add breadcrumbs, Parmesan, parsley, garlic salt, and seasoning salt in a third bowl and mix well.
2. Line baking sheet with wax paper. Set aside.
3. Cut mozzarella pieces in half vertically so that you will end up with 16 mozzarella sticks. Then, for each piece, dredge first in flour, followed by egg wash, and third in breadcrumb mixture. Dredge again in egg wash and breadcrumbs for a thicker coat. Place pieces on prepared baking sheet and place in freezer for at least 1 hour or overnight.
4. To prepare mozzarella sticks preheat deep fryer to 350°F.

5. About 4 sticks at a time, deep fry for about 30 seconds or until golden brown. Using a slotted spoon, transfer to a rack or plate lined with paper towels to drain.
6. Serve warm with marinara sauce.

Nutrition:
Calories: 118 Fat: 7 g Saturated Fat: 4 g Carbs: 8 g Sugar: 1g Protein: 7 g Sodium: 340 mg

Waffle House's Waffle

Preparation Time: 5 minutes

Cooking Time: 20 minutes

Servings: 6

Ingredients

- 11/2cups of all-purpose flour
- 1 teaspoon of salt
- 1/2teaspoon of baking soda
- 1 egg
- 1/2cup + 1 tablespoon of granulated white sugar
- 2 tablespoons of butter, softened
- 2 tablespoons of shortening
- 1/2cup of half-and-half
- 1/2cup of milk
- 1/4cup of buttermilk
- 1/4teaspoon of vanilla

Directions

1. Prepare the dry mixture by sifting the flour into a bowl and mixing it with soda's salt and bicarbonate.

2. In a medium bowl, lightly beat an egg when the egg has become frothy, hammer in the butter, sugar, and shortening.

3. When the mixture is thoroughly mixed, hammer in the half-and-half, vanilla, milk, and buttermilk, continue beating the mixture until it's smooth.

4. While beating the wet mixture, slowly pour in the dry mix to combine thoroughly and take away all the lumps.

5. Chill the batter overnight (optional but recommended; if you can't chill the mixture overnight, leave it for 15 to twenty minutes).

6. Take the batter out of the refrigerator. Preheat and grease your waffle iron.

7. Cook each waffle for 3 to four minutes. Serve with butter and syrup.

Nutrition:

Calories 313.8, Total Fat 12.4g, Carbohydrates 45g, Protein 5.9g Sodium 567.9mg

Burrito

Preparation Time: 15 minutes
Cooking Time: 20 minutes
Servings: 10

Ingredients:

- 1 pound pork sausage mild
- 1/2 cup yellow onion diced
- 1/4 cup fresh tomatoes diced
- One tablespoon of green chilies
- 10 — tortillas
- Nine eggs
- 6 ounces American cheese 12 sliced pieces
- 1/2 cup salsa

Directions:

1. Crumble and fry the pork sausage, stir and break the meat in small parts to cook.
2. Place drained sausage in the frying pan. Add the onion, green chilies and tomatoes, heat up at medium temperature until sausage and vegetables are cooked through. Stir from time to time.
3. Measure and beat 2 cups of eggs. Add the eggs and the sausage mixture to the pan. When finished, take off from the heat.
4. Then place sausages and egg mixture (2 tablespoons) on one tortilla. Break each slice of American cheese into two even portions, then put the cheese onto the sausage mixture, and roll the tortilla.
5. If you do all of these ahead of time, you can wrap them in plastic to put them in the refrigerator or freezer, and then heat them for a moment or two in the microwave.

6. Serve with the taco or picante sauce, as you like. You will find these are milder for breakfast and very significant.

Nutrition

Calories: 269 kcal, Carbohydrates: 3 g, Protein: 15 g, Fat: 21 g, Saturated Fat: 8 g, Cholesterol: 196

Margarita

Preparation Time: 1 minute

Cooking Time: 0 minutes

Servings 1

Ingredients

- 11/2ounce of Cuervo or 1800 gold tequila
- 3/4 ounce of Cointreau
- 3/4 ounce of Grand Marnier
- 1/2ounce of lime juice
- 2 ounces of sour mix
- Ice, for serving

Directions

1. Refrigerate (or even freeze) the glass you plan to use.
2. While chilling, mix all the ingredients in a shaker and shake well.
3. If you wish salt on your margarita rim, pour some sea salt on a little dish, wet the rim of your chilled glass, and read the salt.
4. Add some ice, and pour the margarita mixture in.

Nutrition:

Calories: 153 Total Fat: 0g Carbs:7g Protein: 0.2g Fiber:0.2g

Applebee's Triple Chocolate Meltdown

Preparation time: 25 minutes

Cooking time: 8 minutes

Servings: 2–3

Ingredients

- 4 ounces semisweet chocolate chips
- 1/2cup butter
- 2 large whole eggs
- 2 large egg yolks
- 1/4cup sugar, plus more for dusting
- 2 tablespoons of all-purpose flour
- 1/4teaspoon salt

Toppings

- 4 ounces white chocolate
- 4 ounces semisweet chocolate
- 2 teaspoons vegetable shortening, divided
- 4 scoops vanilla ice cream

Directions

1. Preheat oven to 400°F. Grease muffin pans or ramekins and mud with sugar. Melt chocolate chips with butter over a double saucepan, whisking until smooth.

2. In a separate bowl, whisk together the entire eggs, yolks, and sugar until light and fluffy.

3. Whisk both mixtures together.

4. Gradually add flour and salt, whisking until blended.

5. Distribute evenly into prepared pans and arrange on a baking sheet.

6. Bake until edges are done, and centers are still soft (about 8 minutes).

7. Invert onto plate.

8. Prepare toppings. Place each sort of chocolate in separate, microwave-safe bowls. Add a teaspoon of shortening to every bowl and cook in the microwave for about 15 seconds and stir. Repeat until smooth.

9. Top the cake pieces with frozen dessert and drizzle with melted chocolate.

Nutrition

Calories 727, Total Fat 31 g, Carbohydrates 107 g, Protein 11 g, Sodium 562 mg

Pei Wei's Thai Chicken Satay

Preparation Time: 10 minutes
Cooking time: 30 minutes
Servings: 4

Ingredients:

- 1-pound boneless, skinless chicken thighs
- 6-inch bamboo skewers, soaked in water
- Thai satay marinade - 1 tablespoon coriander seeds
- 1 teaspoon cumin seeds
- 2 teaspoons chopped lemongrass
- 1 teaspoon salt   - 1 teaspoon turmeric powder
- 1/4teaspoon roasted chili
- 1/2cup coconut milk
- 11/2tablespoons light brown sugar
- 1 teaspoon lime juice
- 2 teaspoons fish sauce
- Peanut sauce
- 2 tablespoons soy sauce
- 1 tablespoon rice wine vinegar
- 2 tablespoons brown sugar - 1/4cup peanut butter
- 1 teaspoon chipotle Tabasco
- Whisk all ingredients until well incorporated. Store in an airtight container in the refrigerator. Will last for 3 days.
- Thai sweet cucumber relish - 1/4cup white vinegar
- 3/4 cup sugar - 3/4 cup water
- 1 tablespoon ginger, minced
- 1 Thai red chili, minced - 1 medium cucumber

- 1 tablespoon toasted peanuts, chopped

Directions:

1. Cut any excess fat from the chicken, then cut into strips about 3 inches long and 1 inch wide. Thread the strips onto the skewers.
2. Prepare the Thai Satay Marinade and the Peanut Sauce in separate bowls by simply whisking together all of the ingredients for each.
3. Dip the chicken skewers in the Thai Satay Marinade and allow to marinate for at least 4 hours. Reserve the marinade when you remove the chicken skewers.
4. You can either cook the skewers on the grill, basting with the marinade halfway through, or you can do the same in a 350-degree F oven. They taste better on the grill.
5. To prepare the Cucumber Relish, simply add all of the ingredients together and stir to make sure the cucumber is coated.
6. When the chicken skewers are done cooking, serve with peanut sauce and the cucumber relish.

Nutrition:

Calories 404, Total Fat 12 g, Carbs 59 g, Protein 8 g, Sodium 436 mg

Baked Potatoes with Bacon

Preparation Time: 5 minutes
Cooking Time: 30 minutes
Servings: 4

Ingredients:

- 4 potatoes, scrubbed, halved, cut lengthwise
- 1 tbsp. olive oil
- Salt and black pepper to taste
- 4 oz. bacon, chopped

Directions:

1. Preheat air fryer to 390 °F. Brush the potatoes with olive oil and season with salt and pepper. Arrange them in the greased frying basket, cut-side down.
2. Bake for 15 minutes, flip them, top with bacon and bake for 12-15 minutes or until potatoes are golden and bacon is crispy. Serve warm.

Nutrition:
Calories: 150 Carbs: 9 g Fat: 7 g Protein: 12 g

Asparagus & Lemon Bruschetta

Preparation Time: 5 minutes
Cooking Time: 10 minutes
Servings: 2

Ingredients:

- 5 bruschetta toast, prepared
- 5 tablespoons cheese & prosciutto spread
- 1/4 cup asparagus, cooked & sliced
- 2 tablespoons chive and lemon vinaigrette
- 5 bits lemon zest

Cheese & Prosciutto Spread:

- 1/4 cup ricotta cheese
- 1 1/3 Oz cheese, room temperature
- 1 1/3 Oz mascarpone cheese
- 1/4 cup prosciutto cheese
- 1/4 teaspoon garlic puree
- 1/2 tablespoon lemon juice
- Pinch of salt & pepper

Chive & Lemon Vinaigrette:

- 1 1/2 tablespoons corn syrup
- 4 tablespoons lemon juice
- 1 tablespoon chives, chopped
- 3/4 cup vegetable oil
- Pinch salt & pepper

Directions:

1. To make the vinaigrette: Combine the corn syrup and lemon juice in a food processor for 1 minute.
2. Turn the blender to high speed and pour vegetable oil slowly through the top of the blender until it is fully integrated. Add Chives, then mix for 2 seconds. Set it aside for assembly.
3. The cheese spread preparation: blend the ricotta cheese and cream cheese in a small mixer for 4-5 minutes or until smooth at speed 2.
4. Add the mascarpone cheese, garlic puree, and prosciutto, then blend for 1 or 2 minutes more. Put aside for assembly.
5. To assemble the bruschetta: Par cook toast in the oven at 525 degrees for 1 minute or until golden brown. Put 1 lb. of the cheese and spread the prosciutto on each slice of toast.
6. Melt the cheese on the bruschetta for 2 1/2 minutes or until golden brown, in a 525-degree oven.
7. Put it into your serving plate. Mix the sliced asparagus and 1 tablespoon of lemon vinaigrette, lemon zest, and salt and pepper season in a small mixing cup.
8. Place the toast on top of each bruschetta – piling it high and clean. Drizzle 1 spoonful of lemon vinaigrette around and over the toast.

Nutrition:

Calories: 592, Total Fat: 42g Cholesterol: 138mg, Sodium: 436mg, Potassium: 270mg,

Pasta and Soups Recipes

Three Cheese Chicken Penne from Applebee's

Preparation Time: 10 minutes
Cooking Time: 1 hour
Servings: 4

Ingredients:

- 2 boneless skinless chicken breasts
- 1 cup Italian salad dressing
- 3 cups penne pasta
- 6 tablespoons olive oil, divided
- 15 ounces Alfredo sauce
- 8 ounces combination mozzarella, Parmesan, and provolone cheeses, grated
- 4 roma tomatoes, seeded and diced
- 4 tablespoons fresh basil, diced
- 2 cloves garlic, finely chopped
- Shredded parmesan cheese for serving

Directions:

1. Preheat oven to 350°F.
2. In a bowl, add chicken then drizzle with Italian dressing. Mix to coat chicken with dressing fully. Cover using plastic wrap and keep inside refrigerator overnight but, if you're in a hurry, at least 2 hours is fine.
3. Follow instructions on package to cook penne pasta. Drain, then set aside.
4. Brush 3 tablespoons oil onto grates of grill then preheat to medium-high heat. Add marinated chicken onto grill, discarding the marinade.

Cook chicken until both sides are fully cooked and internal temperature measures 165°F. Remove from grill. Set aside until cool enough to handle. Then, cut chicken into thin slices.

5. In a large bowl, add cooked noodles, Alfredo sauce, and grilled chicken. Mix until combined.
6. Drizzle remaining oil onto large casserole pan, then pour noodle mixture inside. Sprinkle cheeses on top. Bake for about 15-20 minutes or until cheese turns a golden and edges of mixture begins to bubble. Remove from oven.
7. Mix tomatoes, basil, and garlic in a bowl. Add on top of pasta.
8. Sprinkle parmesan cheese before serving.

Nutrition:
Calories 308, Total Fat 34 g, Carbs 18 g, Protein 17 g,

Olive Garden's Fettuccine Alfredo

Preparation Time: 5 minutes
Cooking Time: 25 minutes
Servings: 6

Ingredients:

- 1/2cup butter, melted
- 2 tablespoons cream cheese
- 1 pint heavy cream 1 teaspoon garlic powder
- Some salt
- Some black pepper
- 2/3 cup parmesan cheese, grated
- 1 pound fettuccine, cooked

Directions:

1. Melt the cream cheese in the melted butter over medium heat until soft.
2. Add the heavy cream and season the mixture with garlic powder, salt, and pepper.
3. Reduce the heat to low and allow the mixture to simmer for another 15 to 20 minutes.
4. Remove the mixture from heat and add in the parmesan. Stir everything to melt the cheese.
5. Pour the sauce over the pasta and serve.

Nutrition:

Calories 330, Total Fat 29 g, Carbs 34 g, Protein 12 g,

Spaghetti Frittata

Preparation Time: 5 minutes
Cooking Time: 30 minutes
Servings: 6

Ingredients:

- 1/2cup chopped green pepper or 1/2cup chopped onion
- 2 tablespoons olive oil
- 1 tablespoon butter
- 1/4cup milk
- 2 cups grated Parmesan cheese
- 1/2teaspoon dried basil leaves
- 1 cup cooked spaghetti or fettuccine cut into 5 cm pieces
- 6 eggs

Directions:

1. Heat the olive oil and butter in a pan until it melts.
2. Add the green pepper and cook over medium heat, stirring frequently until tender and crispy at the same time.
3. Meanwhile, in a large bowl, mix the eggs with the milk, 1/4cup grated Parmesan cheese, salt and pepper, and basil.
4. Add the cooked pasta to the egg mixture and stir gently.
5. Next, add the egg mixture to the pan and arrange the pasta in a uniform layer.
6. Cook the egg mixture over medium heat, raising the sides with a spatula occasionally so that the raw egg flows underneath.
7. When the egg mixture is almost ready, but still moist, after 10 minutes, cover it with grated Parmesan cheese. Cook for a few more

minutes until it begins to brown. Remove from the oven and cut the frittata into pieces. Serve immediately.

Nutrition:

Calories 350, Total Fat 24 g, Carbs 14 g, Protein 17 g,

Outback's Baked Potato Soup

Preparation Time: 5 minutes

Cooking Time: 40 minutes

Servings: 8

Ingredients

- 2 quarts water
- 8 medium-sized potatoes, cut into chunks
- 4 cans of chicken broth
- 1 small onion, minced
- 1 teaspoon salt
- 1 teaspoon of ground pepper
- 2 cups of cold water
- 1 cup of butter
- 3/4 cup of flour
- 1 1/2 cup of heavy cream
- 1 1/2 cups of jack cheese
- 2-3 thick-cut bacon slices, cooked and diced
- 1/4 cup of green onion, minced

Directions

1. In a pot, add water and potatoes. Bring back a boil, reduce heat to medium, and cook potatoes for 10-15 minutes or tender. Drain and put aside.

2. In a separate pot, pour in broth and blend in onions, salt, pepper, and water. Simmer for 20 minutes.

3. Meanwhile, in another pot, whisk together butter and flour. Slowly add this to the pan of broth. Stir in cream to the mixture and simmer for 20 minutes. Mix in potatoes to reheat.

4. Sprinkle jack cheese, bacon bits, and green onions on top. Serve.

Nutrition:

Calories: 845, Total Fat: 49 g, Carbs: 81 g, Protein: 23 g,
Sodium: 1652 mg

Macaroni and Cheese

Preparation Time: 10 minutes

Cooking time: 30 minutes

Servings: 3

Ingredients:

- 2 tablespoons butter
- 2 tablespoons flour
- 1 teaspoon salt
- 1 teaspoon dry mustard
- 21/2cups milk
- 1/2pound (about 2 cups) cheddar (divided)
- 1/2pound (2 cups) elbow macaroni, cooked

Directions:

1. Preheat the oven to 375°F.
2. Melt the butter in a saucepan, then stir in the flour, salt, and mustard.
3. Whisk in the milk and stir constantly until the sauce begins to thicken.
4. Stir in 11/2cups of the cheese. Continue to stir until melted, then remove from the heat.
5. Add the cooked elbow macaroni and the cheese sauce to a buttered casserole dish. Stir until the macaroni is covered with sauce. Top with the remaining cheese and bake for 25 minutes or until the top is browned and the cheese is bubbly.

Nutrition:

Calories 115 Protein 35 Carbs 26 Fat 5

Chicken Enchilada Soup from Chili's

Preparation Time: 10 minutes

Cooking Time: 50 minutes

Servings: 8

Ingredients

- 1-pound of chicken breast, boneless and skinless, cut in half
- 1 tablespoon of vegetable oil
- 1/2cup of onion, chopped
- 1 garlic clove, finely chopped
- 1-quart chicken broth
- 1 cup of masa harina
- 3 cups of water, divided
- 1 cup of enchilada sauce
- 2 cups of cheddar cheese, grated
- 1 teaspoon of salt
- 1 teaspoon of chili powder
- 1/2teaspoon of ground cumin
- Crispy tortilla strips for garnish

Directions

1. Heat oil in a pot over medium heat. Add chicken breasts and evenly cook until browned on all sides. Remove from pot. Shred, then put aside.

2. Return pot to heat and add onion and garlic. Sauté until onions are translucent. Add chicken stock.

3. Mix masa harina and a couple of cups water in a bowl, then add in the pot with the onions and garlic. Add the remaining water, enchilada sauce, cheddar, salt, flavorer, and cumin. Bring mixture to a boil.

4. Add cooked chicken to the pot and lower heat. Simmer for about 30 to 40 minutes until soup is thick.

5. Garnish with crispy tortilla strips and serve.

Nutrition:

Calories: 290 - Total fat: 16 g - Saturated fat: 9 g Carbs: 14 g - Sugar: 1 g Fibers: 2 g - Protein: 22 g -Sodium: 512 mg

Veggie Lo Mein

Preparation Time: 10 minutes
Cooking Time: 5 minutes
Servings: 4

Ingredients:

- 1-large onion
- 2 tsp. fresh ginger
- 8 oz. whole-grain spaghetti
- 10 oz. frozen chopped broccoli
- 1 1/2 c. frozen shelled edamame
- 2 cups shredded carrots
- 10 oz. baby spinach
- 2 tbsp. toasted sesame oil
- 1/4 cup lower-sodium soy sauce
- 2 tbsp. balsamic vinegar
- 4-large eggs

Directions:

1. Cut a 1-broad onion in thin slices. 2 teaspoons of fresh ginger peel and grate. Put away. Cook 8 ounces of whole-grain spaghetti in a large pot of boiling water as directed by the label.
2. Before draining, add 10 ounces of frozen broccoli, 1 1/2 cups of frozen edamame shelled, 2 cups of carrots, and 10 ounces of spinach for children. Drain well; put away.
3. Heat 2 table cubits of toasted sesame oil on medium-high in the same pot. Slice the onion over and cook for 5 minutes.

4. Put the fresh ginger grated peeled, 1/4 cup lower-sodium soy sauce, and 2-tbsp. of balsamic vinegar. Cook on for 1 minute.
5. Beat four big eggs in a small pot. Add eggs to the dish, and cook without stirring for 2 minutes. Attach the pot and cook the noodle mixture, turning, for 2 minutes or until heated through.

Nutrition:

Calories: 460 Fiber 15 g Carbs: 63 g Sodium: 785 mg Protein: 25 g Fat: 15 g (3 g Sat)

Sides and Salads Recipes

Clams Bruschetta

Preparation Time: 15 minutes
Cooking Time: 2 minutes
Servings: 8

Ingredients:

- 8 slices Italian bread
- 1 clove garlic, halved 1/2cup extra virgin olive oil
- 1 cup (or 2 6-ounce cans) chopped clam meat, drained
- 4 ripe tomatoes, cut into slices
- Salt and freshly ground pepper to taste
- 12 fresh arugula or basil leaves, rinsed and dried

Directions:

1. Preheat grill, then toast both sides of the bread slices.
2. Rub the garlic onto each side of the bread to infuse with flavor.
3. Place a tomato slice and some clam meat on each bread slice. Sprinkle with salt and pepper to taste. Drizzle olive oil on top.
4. Cut arugula or basil thinly and place onto bruschetta. Serve.

Nutrition:

Calories: 424.4 Total Fat 29.4 g cholesterol 19.3 mg Sodium 276.8 mg
Total Carbohydrate 29.1 g Dietary Fiber 3.4 g Sugar: 5.2 g
Protein 12.6 g

Glazed Carrots

Preparation Time: 10 minutes
Cooking time: 35 minutes
Servings: 3

Ingredients:
- 2 pounds baby carrots, rinsed
- 1 teaspoon salt
- 1/4cup brown sugar
- 2 tablespoons butter

Directions:
1. Place the carrots in a saucepan and add enough water just to cover them.
2. Bring to a boil, then reduce heat, cover and simmer for about 35 minutes or until the carrots are fork-tender.
3. Remove approximately half of the water from the saucepan, then add the butter, salt, and brown sugar. Cover and allow to cook for about 5 more minutes.

Nutrition:
Calories 118, Total Fat 90 g, Carbs 66 g, Protein 39 g, Sodium 2038 mg

Chicken BBQ Salad

Preparation time: 40 minutes
Cooking Time: 15 minutes
Serving: 4

Ingredients:

- 1 large boneless, skinless chicken breast
- 3 tablespoon ranch dressing
- 1 can of black beans
- Large head of romaine lettuce
- 1 cup of corn kernels, fresh or frozen
- 3 tablespoon barbecue sauce plus more for marinating and drizzling
- 1 cup tri-color tortilla strips

Directions:

1. Place the chicken breast in a large zip-lock bag & add in the barbecue sauce; enough to cover the meat. Seal & let marinate for half an hour.
2. Preheat your grill over medium high heat.
3. Rinse the black beans, chop the romaine lettuce & heat a grill pan over medium high heat.
4. For dressing: Combine barbecue sauce together with ranch to taste.
5. Spray the grill with non-stick grilling spray & place the marinated chicken breast over the grill. Grill until the chicken is completely cooked through & juices run clear, for six minutes per side.
6. In the meantime, add corn to the grill pan. Lightly sprinkle with smoked paprika & grill until a few kernels are blackened slightly.
7. Let the chicken to rest for a few minutes and then dice into small bite-sized pieces.

8. Add romaine together with chicken, black beans, tortilla strips and corn in a large serving bowl. Add dressing; toss until evenly coated. Drizzle more of barbecue sauce on top of the ingredients, if desired. Serve immediately & enjoy.

Nutrition:

Calories 218, Total Fat 24 g, Carbs 14 g, Protein 17 g,

Brussels Sprouts N' Kale Salad

Preparation Time: 5 minutes
Cooking Time: 0 minutes
Servings: 6

Ingredients:

- 1 bunch kale
- 1 pound Brussels sprouts
- 1/4cup craisins (or dry cranberries)
- 1/2cup pecans, chopped

Maple vinaigrette:

- 1/2cup olive oil
- 1/4cup apple cider vinegar
- 1/4cup maple syrup
- 1 teaspoon dry mustard

Directions:

1. Slice the kale and Brussels sprouts with a cheese grater or mandolin slicer. Transfer to a salad bowl.
2. Add the pecans to a skillet on high heat. Toast for 60 seconds, then transfer to the salad bowl.
3. Add the craisins.
4. Mix all of the ingredients for the vinaigrette and whisk to combine.
5. Pour the vinaigrette over the salad and toss. Refrigerate for a few hours or preferably overnight before serving.

Nutrition:

Calories 211, Total Fat 6 g, Carbs 4 g, Protein 7 g,

House Salad and Dressing

Preparation Time: 10 minutes

Cooking Time: 0

Servings: 12

Ingredients:

Salad

- 1 head iceberg lettuce
- 1/4small red onion, sliced thin
- 6–12 black olives, pitted
- 6 pepperoncini
- 2 small roma tomatoes, sliced
- Croutons
- 1/4cup shredded or grated romano or parmesan cheese

Dressing:

- 1 packet Italian dressing mix
- 3/4 cup vegetable/canola oil
- 1/4cup olive oil
- 1 tablespoon mayonnaise
- 1/3 cup white vinegar
- 1/4cup water
- 1/2teaspoon sugar
- 1/2teaspoon dried Italian seasoning
- 1/2teaspoon salt
- 1/4teaspoon pepper
- 1/4teaspoon garlic powder

Directions:

1. To make the dressing, combine all ingredients in a small bowl. Thoroughly whisk together. Refrigerate for 1 hour to marinate.
2. Add the salad ingredient to a salad bowl. When ready to serve, add some of the dressing to the salad and toss to coat. Add grated cheese as a garnish as desired.
3. Store remaining dressing in an airtight container. Keep refrigerated and it can be stored for up to 3 weeks.

Nutrition:

Calories 221 - Total Fat 4 g - Carbs 5 g - Protein 7 g,

Fennel and Orange Salad

Preparation Time: 15 minutes
Cooking Time: 0 minute
Servings: 6

Ingredients:

- 4 navel oranges, peeled, halved, and thinly sliced
- 3 fennel bulbs, trimmed and thinly sliced, fronds reserved for garnish
- 2 tbsp. extra-virgin olive oil
- 1 tbsp. white wine vinegar
- Salt
- Freshly ground black pepper

Directions:

1. In a prepared large bowl, combine the orange and fennel slices. In a small bowl, whisk together the olive oil and vinegar. Season with salt and pepper.
2. Pour the dressing over the orange and fennel and toss to combine. Roughly chop the fennel fronds and sprinkle them on top.

Nutrition:
Calories: 122 Fat: 5 g Protein: 2 g Carbs: 20 g

Pizzas Recipes

New York Style

Serves:8

Preparation Time: 15 minutes

Cooking Time: 8-10 minutes

Ingredients

- 1 12- to 14-inch tossed pizza crust
- 1/2-1 cup marinara sauce
- 1/2 teaspoon dried oregano flakes
- 2 cups (8 ounces) medium dry mozzarella, shredded
- 2 Tablespoons parmesan,grated

Directions

1. Preheat oven to 500 degree F.
2. Shred or grate all the cheeses.
3. Spread sauce over the dough, leaving about 1/2 inch free from the edge.
4. Sprinkle oregano flakes over sauce.
5. Cover with shredded mozzarella, followed by grated parmesan.
6. Bake until golden brown and bubbly (about 8-10 minutes).
7. Let rest for cheese to set (about 3-5 minutes).
8. Slice and serve.

Nutrition:

Calories 292 Carbs 22 g Fat 15 g Protein 16 g Sodium 550 mg

Apple Pie Pizza

Servings: 6-8

Preparation Time: 20 minutes

Cooking Time: 17-22 minutes

Ingredients

- 1 thin or pan pizza crust dough

- Cinnamon streusel topping:
- 1/2 cup packed light brown sugar
- 1/2 cup all-purpose flour
- 3/4 teaspoon cinnamon
- 4 tablespoons butter, softened

Apple topping:

- 1 tablespoon butter
- 2 apples, peeled, cored and chopped
- 2 Tablespoons brown sugar
- 1/2 teaspoon cinnamon

For glaze:

- 2 tablespoons butter
- 1/3 cup milk
- 1/4 teaspoon vanilla
- 2 cups powdered sugar

Directions

1. Preheat the oven to 425 degrees F.

2. Par-bake crust just to set dough (about 5 minutes). Remove from oven and let cool.

3. Prepare streusel topping. Combine sugar, flour and cinnamon well and the cut butter in with pastry cutter or fingers. It should have a coarse, cornmeal-like texture. Set aside.

4. Prepare the apple mixture. Melt the butter in a skillet over medium heat. Add apples, brown sugar and cinnamon. While stirring frequently, cook until mixture begins to bubbly and fragrant (about 5 minutes).

5. Remove from heat and let cool slightly.

6. Spread apple mixture over crust and sprinkle with streusel topping.

7. Bake until golden and bubbly (about 12-15 minutes).

8. Remove from oven and let cool on a wire rack.

9. Prepare glaze. Heat milk with butter in a saucepan over medium low to medium heat. Remove from heat as soon as butter is melted and stir in vanilla. Continue whisking while adding sugar gradually until smooth.

10. Drizzle over apple pie pizza and serve.

Nutrition:

Calories 398 Carbs 87 g Fat 8 g Protein 4 g Sodium 209 mg

Deep Dish

Serves:8

Preparation Time: 20 minutes plus 4-6 hours resting time

Cooking Time: 5 minutes

Ingredients

- 1 1/2 teaspoons active dry yeast
- 1 Tablespoon sugar or honey
- 3/4 cup lukewarm water
- 1 1/2 cups all-purpose flour, plus more for dusting
- 1/2 cup semolina flour (optional; if not using, add 1/2 cup all-purpose flour)
- 1/2 teaspoon salt
- 1/8 teaspoon cream of tartar
- 2/3 corn oil plus more for greasing
- 2 Tablespoons butter, softened (optional)

Directions

1. In a small bowl, dissolve yeast and sugar in lukewarm water. Let sit for 15 minutes.
2. In a large bowl, whisk flour(s), salt and cream of tartar together.
3. Make a well and pour in the yeast mixture and oil.
4. Using a mixer with hook attachment, mix briefly to moisten (about 1 minutes)
5. Knead for a short while (2 minutes) to get a shortbread-type texture when baked.

6. Cover with a towel or cling wrap and let rise for 4-6 hours. You may need to oil the dough to avoid crusting, depending on the humidity in your area.

7. Preheat oven to 450 degrees F. Grease pan (You may use a 9 1/2-inch deep-dish pie pan, springform pan or 10-inch cast iron pan).

8. Punch down dough, cover and let rest (15 minutes).

9. Roll out and place in greased pan or press down with hands over pan (Dough will be sticky; dust with flour for easier handling).

10. Bake just until set and matte in appearance (about 5 minutes).

11. Brush dough with butter, if using.

12. Add desired toppings and sauce and bake until golden brown (about 35-40 minutes).

Nutrition:

Calories 282 Carbs 25.7 g Fat 18.4 g Protein 3.9 g Sodium 148 mg

Steamed White Clam Pizza

Servings: 2-4

Preparation Time: 2 hours 15 minutes

Cooking Time: 10-12 minutes

Ingredients

- 1 thin crust pizza dough
- 3/4 cup chopped clams, drained well
- 4 garlic cloves, minced
- 1 Tablespoon dried oregano
- 1/2 cup extra virgin olive oil
- 3/4 cup Pecorino Romano cheese, grated

Directions

1. Preheat the oven to 400°F.
2. Gently mix together drained clams, olive oil, garlic and oregano. Spread evenly over crust.
3. Sprinkle with cheese.
4. Bake until golden brown (about 10–15 minutes).

Nutrition:

Calories 300 Carbs 8 g Fat 12 g Protein 45 g Sodium 300mg

Creamy Bacon

Servings: 6-8
Preparation Time: 15 minutes
Cooking Time: 15-25 minutes

Ingredients

- 1 pizza crust of choice
- 1/2-3/4 cup creamy white sauce with garlic
- 1 cup ricotta
- 6-8 strips bacon, fried crisp, drained on paper towels and chopped
- 1 Tablespoon bacon drippings
- 1/2 cup mushrooms, sliced thinly
- Freshly-ground black pepper, to taste
- Dried thyme (optional)

Directions

1. Preheat oven to 475 degrees F.
2. Bake crust until lightly golden (about 10-15 minutes). Remove from oven and let cool.
3. Heat bacon drippings in a skillet over medium heat and sauté mushrooms until tender and lightly browned (about 3-4 minutes). Remove from heat and drain on paper towels. Let cool slightly.
4. Spread sauce and ricotta over crust.
5. Top with mushroom and bacon.
6. Season with black pepper and sprinkle with thyme (if using).
7. Bake to heat through and brown crust (about 2-5 minutes).
8. Serve immediately.

Nutrition:

Calories 393 Carbs 34 g Fat 22 g Protein 15 g Sodium 434 mg

Classic Pepperoni

Servings: 8
Preparation Time: 15 minutes
Cooking Time: 12-15 minutes

Ingredients

- 1 thin crust pizza dough, or any dough of choice
- 1/2-3/4 basic pizza or marinara sauce
- 2 cups mozzarella, freshly shredded
- 6 ounces pepperoni

Directions

1. Preheat oven to 500 degrees F.
2. Spread sauce over crust.
3. Sprinkle with cheese.
4. Top with mozzarella.
5. Bake until golden and bubbly (about 12-15 minutes).

Nutrition:

Calories 276 Carbs 25 g Fat 14 g Protein 12 g Sodium 656 mg

Sausage, Pepper & Onion Pizza

Preparation Time: 10 minutes
Cooking Time: 40 minutes
Servings: 2

Ingredients:

- Cornmeal or flour, for dusting
- 3 tbsp. extra-virgin olive oil, plus more as needed
- ¾ pound sweet Italian sausage (3 sausages)
- 1 medium yellow onion, sliced
- 1 red bell pepper, cut into ½-inch strips
- 1 green bell pepper, cut into ½-inch strips
- 2 garlic cloves, minced
- ¼ tsp. red pepper flakes
- Simply Amazing Pizza Dough (here) or Pro Dough (here)
- New York–Style Pizza Sauce (here)
- 1 1/3 cups grated mozzarella cheese
- 1 tsp. fine sea salt
- 1/8 tsp. freshly ground black pepper
- ½ tsp. dried oregano

Directions:

1. Preheat the oven and (if using) pizza stone set to 500 °F. Dust a pizza peel with cornmeal (if using a pizza stone), or brush two baking sheets with olive oil.
2. In a large skillet over medium heat, heat the olive oil until it shimmers. Add the sausages and cook until they are browned

on all sides and register 160 °F on an instant-read thermometer, about 8 minutes total. Transfer to a cutting board.

3. Add the onion to the hot pan (adding more oil if necessary), and sauté over medium heat until translucent, about 4 minutes. Add the red and green bell peppers. Sauté the mixture until the onions turn golden, about 4 minutes more, and then add the garlic and red pepper flakes. Cook, stirring, for about 2 additional minutes to infuse the mixture with the garlic. Using a slotted spoon, transfer the mixture to a small bowl.

4. Cut the sausages into ¼-inch-thick slices.

5. Roll out to form one of the dough balls to the desired size, and place it on the prepared peel or baking sheet.

6. Leaving a 1-inch border, spread half of the sauce evenly over the dough. Sprinkle half of the grated mozzarella over the pizza and then arrange half of the sausage slices on top. Spread half of the peppers and onions evenly overall.

7. Bake until the cheese has melted and the crust has browned, 5 to 7 minutes on the pizza stone or 7 to 10 minutes on the baking sheet.

8. Move the pizza put into a cutting board and season with the salt, pepper, and dried oregano. Let it rest for 5 minutes, then slice and serve.

9. Repeat with the remaining dough ball and toppings.

Nutrition:
Calories: 466 Carbs: 12.16 g Cholesterol: 53 mg Fat: 23.45 g
Protein: 52.57 g Sodium: 2875 mg

Main Courses Recipes

PF Chang's Kung Pao Shrimp

Preparation Time: 10 minutes

Cooking time 10 minutes

Servings 4

Ingredients

- 1/4cup of soy sauce
- 1/2teaspoon of cornstarch
- 2 tablespoons of water
- 1/4teaspoon of sesame oil
- 1/2teaspoon of balsamic vinegar
- 1/2teaspoon of sugar
- Pepper to taste
- 3 tablespoons of hot chili oil
- 3 cloves of garlic, minced
- 1/4onion, roughly chopped
- 16 large shrimp, peeled and deveined
- 1/4cup of roasted peanuts
- 5 scallions, chopped

Directions

1. In a bowl, whisk together the soy, cornstarch, water, vegetable oil, balsamic vinegar, sugar, and pepper. Set aside.
2. Add the recent chili oil to a deep skillet or wok and warmth over medium-high heat.

3. Add the minced garlic and onion and cook for about 2 minutes. If you would like to feature other vegetables, like broccoli or peas, you'll add them now.

4. Cook until the veggies are soft. Add the shrimp and cook for about 2 minutes, then stir in the sauce you made earlier and cooked a touch longer until the sauce thickens. Stir to coat the shrimp, remove the skillet from the warmth and stir in the scallions and peanuts.

5. Serve with rice.

Nutrition:

Calories: 760 Total Fat: 52g Carbs: 39g Protein: 40g Fiber:15g

Teriyaki Filet Medallions

Preparation Time: 15 minutes
Cooking time: 20 minutes
Servings: 4

Ingredients:

- 3 (6-ounce) sirloin or ribeye steaks
- 1 red bell pepper, cut in 1-inch squares
- 1 yellow bell pepper, cut in 1-inch squares
- 1 green pepper, cut in 1-inch squares
- 1 large red onion, outer layers cut in 1-inch squares
- Teriyaki marinade
- 1 cup soy sauce
- 1/2cup Apple Cider Vinegar
- 1/2cup Sugar
- 1/2cup Pineapple Juice
- 2 cloves garlic, minced
- 2 teaspoons fresh ginger, grated
- 1 teaspoon red pepper flakes

Directions:

1. In a mixing bowl, combine the marinade ingredients.
2. Cut the steaks in 1-inch cubes and place them in a resalable bag. Reserve a third of the marinade and pour the rest over the meat. Seal and refrigerate for 4 hours or more, manipulating the bag from time to time.
3. Soak your skewers if they're wooden and heat the grill to medium.
4. Thread the skewers by alternating meat and vegetables.

5. Grill for 5–10 minutes on each side, brushing often with the reserved marinade.

Nutrition:

Calories: 681 Total Fat: 30g Carbs: 32g Protein: 71g Fiber: 0g Protein: 59 g Sodium: 1043 mg

Chicken Potpie

Preparation Time: 10 minutes
Cooking Time: 20 minutes
Servings: 6

Ingredients:
- 2 tablespoons canola oil
- 1 medium onion, chopped
- 1/2 cup all-purpose flour
- 1 teaspoon poultry seasoning
- 1 can (14-1/2 ounces) chicken broth 3/4 cup 2% milk 3 cups cubed cooked chicken
- 2 cups frozen mixed vegetables (about 10 ounces), thawed
- 1 sheet refrigerated pie crust

Directions:
1. Preheat oven to 450°. In a large saucepan, heat oil over medium-high heat. Add onion; cook and stir until tender.
2. Stir in flour and poultry seasoning until blended; gradually whisk in broth and milk. Bring to a boil, stirring constantly; cook and stir 2-3 minutes or until thickened.
3. Stir in chicken and vegetables. Transfer to a greased 9-in. deep-dish pie plate; place crust over filling. Trim, seal, and flute edges. Cut slits in crust.
4. Bake 15-20 minutes or until crust is golden brown and filling is bubbly.

Nutrition:
Calories: 439, Fat: 20g Cholesterol: 73mg, Sodium: 526mg, Carbohydrate: 37g, Protein: 26g

Orange Chicken

Preparation Time: 15 minutes
Cooking Time: 30 minutes
Servings: 6

Ingredients:
Orange sauce:

- 11/2tablespoon soy sauce
- 11/2tablespoon water
- 5 tablespoons sugar
- 5 tablespoons white vinegar
- 3 tablespoons orange zest

Chicken preparation:

- 1 egg
- 11/2teaspoon salt
- White pepper, to taste
- 5 tablespoons grapeseed oil, divided
- 1/2cup + 1 tablespoon cornstarch
- 1/4cup flour
- 1/4cup cold water
- 2 pounds chicken breast, boneless and skinless, chopped
- 1 teaspoon fresh ginger, grated
- 1 teaspoon garlic, finely chopped
- 1/2teaspoon hot red chili pepper, ground
- 1/4cup green onion, sliced
- 1 tablespoon rice wine
- 1/2teaspoon sesame oil
- White rice and steamed broccoli for serving

71

Directions:

1. Mix together Ingredients: for the orange sauce in a bowl. Reserve for future.
2. Add egg, salt, pepper, and 1 tablespoon oil to a separate bowl. Mix well.
3. In another bowl, combine 1/2cup cornstarch and flour. Mix until fully blended.
4. Add remaining cornstarch and cold water in a different bowl. Blend until cornstarch is completely dissolved.
5. Heat 3 tablespoons oil in a large deep skillet or wok over high heat.
6. Coat chicken pieces in egg mixture. Let excess drip off. Then, coat in cornstarch mixture. Cook for at least 3 minutes or until both sides are golden brown and chicken is cooked through. Arrange on a plate lined with paper towels to drain excess oil.
7. In a clean large deep skillet, or wok heat remaining oil on high heat. Lightly sauté ginger and garlic for 30 seconds or until aromatic. Toss in peppers and green onions. Stir-fry vegetables for 1-3 minutes, then pour in rice wine. Mix well before adding orange sauce. Bring to a boil. Mix in cooked chicken pieces, then add cornstarch mixture. Simmer until mixture is thick, then mix in sesame oil.

Nutrition:

Calories: 305 Fat: 5 g Carbs: 27 g Protein: 34 g Sodium: 1024 mg

Fried Chicken

Preparation Time: 20 minutes
Cooking Time: 40 minutes
Servings: 4

Ingredients:
Spice mix:

- 1 tablespoon paprika
- 2 teaspoons onion salt
- 1 teaspoon chili powder
- 1 teaspoon black pepper, ground
- 1/2teaspoon celery salt
- 1/2teaspoon dried sage
- 1/2teaspoon garlic powder
- 1/2teaspoon allspice, ground
- 1/2teaspoon dried oregano
- 1/2teaspoon dried basil
- 1/2teaspoon dried marjoram

Chicken preparation:

- 1 whole chicken, cut into parts
- 2 quarts frying oil
- 1 egg white
- 1 1/2cups all-purpose flour
- 1 tablespoon brown sugar
- 1 tablespoon kosher salt

Directions:

1. Preheat oil in deep fryer to 350°F.
2. In a bowl, mix together Ingredients: for the spice mix. Then, add flour, sugar, and salt. Mix well until fully blended.
3. Coat each chicken piece with egg white, then the flour breading. Make sure that the chicken pieces are well-coated.
4. Transfer to a plate and allow chicken to dry for about 5 minutes.
5. Deep-fry breasts and wings together for about 12 minutes or until the temperature on a meat thermometer inserted in the breast's thickest part reads 165 °F. Do the same with legs and thighs. Usually these parts take 1-2 minutes more to cook.
6. Transfer pieces onto a plate lined with paper towels.
7. Serve.

Nutrition:

Calories: 418 - Fat: 22 g - Carbs: 41 g - Protein: 15 g - Sodium: 1495 mg

Quesadilla Burger

Preparation time: 15 minutes
Cooking time: 15 minutes
Servings: 4

Ingredients:

- 1 1/2pounds ground beef 8 (6-inch) flour tortillas 1 tablespoon butter
- Tex-Mex seasoning for the burgers
- 2 teaspoons ground cumin 2 tablespoons paprika 1 teaspoon black pepper
- 1/2teaspoon cayenne pepper, more or less depending on taste
- 1 teaspoon salt or to taste 1 tablespoon dried oregano

Toppings

- 8 slices pepper jack cheese 4 slices Applewood-smoked bacon, cooked and crumbled
- 1/2cup shredded iceberg lettuce
- Pico de Galo
- 1-2 Roma tomatoes, deseeded and diced thin
- ½-1 tablespoon thinly diced onion (red or yellow is fine) 1-2 teaspoons fresh lime juice
- 1-2 teaspoons fresh cilantro, chopped finely
- 1-2 teaspoons thinly diced jalapeños pepper - Salt and pepper to taste

Tex-Mex ranch dressing

- 1/2cup sour cream 1/2cup ranch dressing such as Hidden Valley
- 1 teaspoon Tex-Mex seasoning 1/4cup mild salsa
- Pepper to taste - For serving (optional) - Guacamole, and sour cream

Directions:

1. In a mixing bowl, combine the Tex-Mex seasoning ingredients and stir to ensure they are well combined.
2. Prepare the fresh Pico de Gallo by mixing all the ingredients in a bowl. Set aside in the refrigerator until ready to use.
3. Prepare the Tex-Mex ranch dressing by mixing all the ingredients in a bowl. Set aside in the refrigerator until ready to use.
4. Add 2 tablespoons of the Tex-Mex seasoning to the ground beef and mix it in, being careful not to overwork the beef or your burgers will be tough. Form into 4 large ¼-inch thick burger patties and cook either on the grill or in a skillet to your preference.
5. Heat a clean skillet over medium-low heat. Butter each of the flour tortillas on one side. Place one butter side down in the skillet. Top with 1 slice of cheese, some shredded lettuce, some Pico de Gallo, some bacon, and then top with a cooked burger. Top the burger with some of the Tex-Mex ranch dressing sauce to taste, some Pico the Gallo, bacon, and another slice of cheese.
6. Cover with another tortilla, butter side up. Cook for about 1 minute or until the tortilla is golden. Then carefully flip the tortilla and cook until the cheese has melted. This step can be done in a sandwich press if you have one. Cut the tortillas in quarters or halves and serve with a side of the Tex-Mex ranch dressing, guacamole, and sour cream, if desired

Nutrition:

Calories: 1330, Total Fat: 93 g, Cholesterol: 240 mg, Sodium: 3000 mg, Total Carbohydrate: 50 g, Dietary Fiber: 6 g, Sugars: 7 g, Protein: 74 g

Texas Roadhouse's Red Chili

Preparation time: 20 minutes
Cooking time: 1 hour
Servings: 6

Ingredients

- 2 tablespoons vegetable oil
- 2 pounds beef chuck, cut into bite-sized cubes
- 1 yellow onion, diced
- 2 cloves garlic, chopped
- 1 1/2teaspoons chili powder
- 1 teaspoon ground cumin
- 1 teaspoon paprika
- 1 teaspoon salt
- 1/2teaspoon black pepper
- 1/4teaspoon red pepper flakes
- 1 tablespoon brown sugar
- 1 1/2cups crushed tomatoes
- 2 teaspoons white vinegar
- 1 (15-ounce) can red kidney beans
- 2 jalapeños, seeded and sliced

Optional for topping

- Shredded cheddar
- Green onions, chopped

Directions

1. In a large pot or Dutch oven, heat the oil and brown the meat well on all sides.

2. Add the onion and cook to soften, and then stir in the garlic and cook until fragrant.
3. Add the chili powder, cumin, paprika, salt, pepper, red pepper flakes, and brown sugar. Mix to combine.
4. Stir in the crushed tomatoes and vinegar. Bring the pot to a simmer, cover, and cook for 30 minutes.
5. Add the kidney beans and jalapeños and cook 10 more minutes.
6. Serve hot with a sprinkle of shredded cheese and green onion.

Nutrition:
Calories 201 - Carbs 2 g - Fat 8.2 g - Protein 9.3 g

Café Rio's Sweet Pork Salad

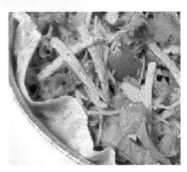

Preparation time: 20 minutes

Cooking time: 5 hours

Servings: 12

Ingredients

- For the Meat
- 6 pounds pork shoulder (yields about 4 pounds cooked, fat removed, shredded pork)
- 1 1/2teaspoons onion salt
- 1/2teaspoon ground black pepper
- 2 cloves garlic, crushed and minced
- 1 can cola (not diet)

For the Sauce

- 2 (4-ounce) cans diced mild to medium green chilies
- 1 1/2cups red enchilada sauce - 1 cup brown sugar
- 2 cloves garlic, chopped - 1 can cola

For the Filling

- Guacamole - Café Rio Black Beans - Cilantro Lime Rice

For Serving (optional)

- 6 corn tortillas, sliced into strips and fried
- 12–16 flour tortillas, softened (or 1 per serving), warmed
- Lettuce, chopped - Tomatoes, sliced
- Sweet onion, sliced - Cheddar or Mexican blend cheese, shredded
- Pico de Gallo OR SALSA - Sour cream - Cilantro, chopped

Directions

1. Preheat the oven to 350°F and place the rack in the bottom third (or use a slow cooker).
2. Season the roast with onion salt and black pepper. Rub the garlic on the top of the meat.
3. Place the roast in the roasting pan (or slow cooker) and pour the cola at the bottom.

4. Cover tightly and roast for 2 hours without opening the oven. Reduce the heat to 200°F and bake 3 more hours. (If using a slow cooker, cook on LOW for 5 hours.)
5. Meanwhile, prepare the black beans and cilantro rice.
6. Remove the meat from the pot and let it cool for about 20 minutes. Remove any visible fat and shred the meat.
7. Drain the pan and place the meat back in it.
8. Prepare the sauce. Place the chilies, enchilada sauce, garlic, and brown sugar in a blender and mix. Add the cola and stir it in with a spoon.
9. Pour the sauce over the meat and jiggle the pan to coat the meat. Place it back in the oven to heat through.
10. To assemble the salad, place a warm flour tortilla on a plate and layer on beans, rice, meat, lettuce, tomato, onion, cheese, guacamole, pico de gallo, sour cream, and cilantro.

Nutrition:

Calories 265 Carbs 2 g Fat 8.2 g Protein 11 g

Chi Chi's Pork Tenderloin

Preparation time: 10 minutes
Cooking time: 15 minutes
Servings: 12

Ingredients

- 2 pounds pork tenderloin
- Chi Chi's Bourbon Marinade
- 10 ounces Chi Chi's diced tomatoes with green chilies, drained
- 1/3 cup bourbon
- 1/3 cup soy sauce
- 1/3 cup Worcestershire sauce
- 1 small yellow onion, chopped
- 2 tablespoons honey
- 2 tablespoons mustard
- 1/2teaspoon red pepper flakes

Directions

1. Combine the ingredients for the marinade and place it in a resealable bag.
2. Add the pork and turn to coat. Refrigerate for 8 hours or overnight, turning it from time to time.
3. Preheat the grill or broiler to medium.
4. Remove the meat from the marinade, reserving the marinade.
5. Grill or broil the meat for 7 minutes on each side, or until it reaches 165°F internally.
6. Strain the marinade into a saucepan and bring it to a boil. Simmer for 2–3 minutes and strain. Serve it as a sauce with the meat.

Nutrition:

Calories 251 Carbs 2 g Fat 8.2 g Protein 10.3 g

Meat Loaf

Preparation Time: 15 minutes
Cooking Time: 1 1/2hours
Servings: 6

Ingredients:
- 2 large eggs
- 2/3 cup whole milk
- 3 slices bread, torn
- 1/2 cup chopped onion
- 1/2 cup grated carrot
- 1 cup shredded cheddar or part-skim mozzarella cheese
- 1 tablespoon minced fresh parsley or
- 1 teaspoon dried parsley
- 1 teaspoon dried basil, thyme, or sage, optional
- 1 teaspoon salt 1/4 teaspoon pepper
- 1-1/2 pounds lean ground beef

TOPPING:
- 1/2 cup tomato sauce 1/2 cup packed brown sugar 1 teaspoon prepared mustard

Directions:
1. In a large bowl, beat eggs. Add milk and bread; let stand until liquid is absorbed. Stir in the onion, carrot, cheese, and seasonings.
2. Crumble beef over mixture and mix well. Shape into a 7-1/2x3-1/2x2-1/2-in. loaf in a shallow baking pan.
3. Bake, uncovered, at 350° for 45 minutes. Combine the topping ingredients, spoon half of the mixture over meat loaf.

4. Bake 30 minutes longer or until meat is no longer pink and a thermometer reads 160°, occasionally spooning remaining topping over loaf. Let stand 10 minutes before serving.
5.

Nutrition:

Calories: 398, Fat: 17g, Saturated fat: 9g, Cholesterol: 164mg,

Grilled Pork Chops

Preparation Time: 20 minutes
Cooking Time: 10 minutes
Servings: 4

Ingredients:
- 1/4 cup kosher salt
- 1/4 cup sugar
- 2 cups water
- 2 cups ice water
- 4 center-cut pork rib chops (1 inch thick and 8 ounces each)
- 2 tablespoons canola oil

Basic Rub:
- 3 tablespoons paprika
- 1 teaspoon each garlic powder, onion powder, ground cumin and ground mustard
- 1 teaspoon coarsely ground pepper
- 1/2 teaspoon ground chipotle pepper

Directions:
1. In a large saucepan, combine salt, sugar and 2 cups water; cook and stir over medium heat until salt and sugar are dissolved. Remove from heat. Add 2 cups ice water to cool brine to room temperature.
2. Place pork chops in a large resealable plastic bag; add cooled brine. Seal bag, pressing out as much air as possible; turn to coat chops. Place in a 13x9-in. baking dish. Refrigerate 8-12 hours. Remove chops from brine, rinse, and pat dry.

3. Discard brine. Brush both sides of chops with oil. In a small bowl, mix rub ingredients; rub over pork chops. Let stand at room temperature 30 minutes.
4. Grill chops on an oiled rack, covered, over medium heat 4-6 minutes on each side or until a thermometer reads 145°. Let stand 5 minutes before serving.

Nutrition:

Calories: 300, Fat: 18g, Cholesterol: 72mg, Sodium: 130mg, Carbohydrate: 5g, Protein: 30g

Golden Eggplant Fries

Preparation Time: 10 minutes
Cooking Time: 15 minutes
Servings: 8

Ingredients:

- 2 eggs
- 2 cups almond flour
- 2 tbsp. coconut oil, spray
- 2 eggplant, peeled and cut thinly
- Sunflower seeds and pepper

Directions:

1. Preheat your oven to 400 °F.
2. Take a bowl and mix with sunflower seeds and black pepper.
3. Take another bowl and beat eggs until frothy.
4. Dip the eggplant pieces into the eggs.
5. Then coat them with the flour mixture.
6. Add another layer of flour and egg.
7. Then, take a baking sheet and grease with coconut oil on top.
8. Bake for about 15 minutes.
9. Serve and enjoy!

Nutrition:
Calories: 212 Fat: 15.8g Carbs: 12.1 g Protein: 8.6 g

Desserts Recipes

Apple Chimi Cheesecake

Preparation Time: 10 minutes
Cooking time: 10 minutes
Servings: 2

Ingredients:

- 2 (9 inch) flour tortillas
- 1/4cup granulated sugar
- 1/2teaspoon cinnamon
- 3 ounces' cream cheese, softened
- 1/2teaspoon vanilla extract
- 1/3 cup apple, peeled and finely chopped
- Oil for frying
- Vanilla ice cream (optional)
- Caramel topping (optional)

Directions:

1. Make sure your tortillas and cream cheese are at room temperature; this will make them both easier to work with.
2. In a small bowl, combine the sugar and cinnamon.
3. In another mixing bowl, combine the cream cheese and vanilla until smooth. Fold in the apple.
4. Divide the apple and cheese mixture in two and place half in the center of each tortilla. Leave at least an inch margin around the outside.
5. Fold the tortilla top to the middle, then the bottom to the middle, and then roll it up from the sides.
6. Heat about half an inch of oil in a skillet over medium heat.
7. Place the filled tortillas into the skillet and fry on each side until they are golden brown. Transfer them to a paper towel lined plate to drain

any excess oil, then immediately coat them with the cinnamon and sugar.

8. Serve with a scoop of ice cream.

Nutrition:
Calories: 267 Fat: 5 g Carbs: 15 g Protein: 18 g Sodium: 276 mg

Chocolate Mousse Dessert Shooter

Preparation Time: 30 minutes
Cooking time: 2 minutes
Servings: 4

Ingredients:

- 2 tablespoons butter
- 6 ounces' semi-sweet chocolate chips (1 cup), divided
- 2 eggs
- 1 teaspoon vanilla
- 8 Oreo cookies
- 1/2cup prepared fudge sauce
- 2 tablespoons sugar
- 1/2cup heavy cream
- Canned whipped cream

Directions:

1. Melt the butter and all but 1 tablespoon of the chocolate chips in a double boiler.
2. When they are melted, stir in the vanilla and remove from the heat.
3. Whisk in the egg yolks.
4. Beat the egg whites until they form soft peaks, and then fold them into the chocolate mixture.
5. Beat the sugar and heavy cream in a separate bowl until it forms stiff peaks or is the consistency that you desire. Fold this into the chocolate mixture.
6. Crush the remaining chocolate chips into small pieces and stir them into the chocolate.
7. Crush the Oreos. (You can either scrape out the cream from the cookies or just crush the entire cookie.)

8. Spoon the cookie crumbs into the bottom of your cup and pat them down. Layer the chocolate mixture on top. Finish with whipped cream and either more chocolate chips or Oreo mixture.
9. Store in the refrigerator until ready to serve.

Nutrition:
Calories: 389 Fat: 11.6 g Carbs: 25. 2 g Protein: 39.0 g Sodium: 222 mg

Cherry Chocolate Cobbler

Preparation Time: 10 minutes
Cooking time: 45 minutes
Servings: 8

Ingredients:
- 11/2cups all-purpose flour
- 1/2cup sugar
- 2 teaspoons baking powder
- 1/2teaspoon salt
- 1/4cup butter
- 6 ounces' semisweet chocolate morsels
- 1/4cup milk
- 1 egg, beaten
- 21 ounces' cherry pie filling
- 1/2cup finely chopped nuts

Directions:
1. Preheat the oven to 350°F.
2. Combine the flour, sugar, baking powder, salt and butter in a large mixing bowl. Use a pastry blender to cut the mixture until there are lumps the size of small peas.
3. Melt the chocolate morsels. Let cool for approximately 5 minutes, then add the milk and egg and mix well. Beat into the flour mixture, mixing completely.
4. Spread the pie filling in a 2-quart casserole dish. Randomly drop the chocolate batter over the filling, then sprinkle with nuts.
5. Bake for 40–45 minutes.
6. Serve with a scoop of vanilla ice cream if desired.

Nutrition:
Calories: 502 Fat: 1.8 g Carbs: 10. 2 g Protein: 19.0 g Sodium: 265 mg

Snickerdoodle Cookies

Preparation Time: 30 minutes
Cooking Time: 2 hours & 5 minutes
Servings: 16

Ingredients:
- 1/2cup butter, softened
- 1/2cup granulated sugar
- 1/3 cup brown sugar
- 1 egg
- 1/2teaspoon vanilla
- 11/2cups flour
- 1/4teaspoon salt
- 1/2teaspoon baking soda
- 1/4teaspoon cream of tartar
- 2 tablespoons granulated sugar
- 1 teaspoon cinnamon

Directions:
1. Preheat oven to 300°F.
2. Using a mixer, combine softened butter and sugars. Mix in egg and vanilla. Combine until there are no longer lumps.
3. Mix flour, salt, baking soda, and cream of tartar in a bowl. Then, combine dry ingredients with wet ingredients. Blend well. Let rest in refrigerator for at least 30 minutes.
4. Mix 2 tablespoons granulated sugar and teaspoon of cinnamon together in a bowl.
5. Ball about 21/2tablespoons dough and coat evenly with cinnamon and sugar mixture. Transfer onto a baking sheet sprayed with cooking spray. Repeat for the rest of the dough.

6. Bake for no longer than 12 minutes. Cookies should be light golden brown but still soft, not crunchy.
7. Serve.

Nutrition:

Calories: 460, Carbohydrates: 65g, Protein: 6g, Fat: 19g, Saturated Fat: 9g,Cholesterol: 37mg, Sodium: 225mg, Potassium: 396mg, Fiber: 3g, Sugar: 20g

Pumpkin Custard with Gingersnaps

Preparation Time: 30 minutes
Cooking time: 35 minutes
Servings: 8

Ingredients:
Custard

- 8 egg yolks
- 1 3/4 cups (1 15-ounce can) pure pumpkin puree
- 1 3/4 cups heavy whipping cream
- 1/2cup sugar
- 11/2teaspoons pumpkin pie spice
- 1 teaspoon vanilla

Topping:
- 1 cup crushed gingersnap cookies
- 1 tablespoon melted butter

Whipped Cream:
- 1 cup heavy whipping cream
- 1 tablespoon superfine sugar (or regular sugar if you have no caster sugar)
- 1/2teaspoon pumpkin pie spice
- Garnish:
- 8 whole gingersnap cookies

Directions:

1. Preheat the oven to 350°F.
2. Separate the yolks from 8 eggs and whisk them together in a large mixing bowl until they are well blended and creamy.
3. Add the pumpkin, sugar, vanilla, heavy cream and pumpkin pie spice and whisk to combine.
4. Cook the custard mixture in a double boiler, stirring until it has thickened enough that it coats a spoon.
5. Pour the mixture into individual custard cups or an 8×8-inch baking pan and bake for about 20 minutes if using individual cups or 30–35 minutes for the baking pan, until it is set, and a knife inserted comes out clean.
6. While the custard is baking, make the topping by combining the crushed gingersnaps and melted butter. After the custard has been in the oven for 15 minutes, sprinkle the gingersnap mixture over the top.
7. When the custard has passed the clean knife test, remove from the oven and let cool to room temperature.
8. Whisk the heavy cream and pumpkin pie spice together with the caster sugar and beat just until it thickens.
9. Serve the custard with the whipped cream and garnish each serving with a gingersnap.

Nutrition:

Calories: 243 Fat: 6.8 g Carbs: 13. 2 g Protein: 17.0 g Sodium: 313 mg

Frozen Lemon & Blueberry

Preparation Time: 30 minutes
Cooking Time: 10 minutes
Servings: 4

Ingredients:

- 6 cup fresh blueberries
- 8 sprigs fresh thyme
- ¾ cup light brown sugar
- 1 tsp .lemon zest
- ¼ cup lemon juice
- 2 cups water

Directions:

1. Add blueberries, thyme, and sugar in a pan over medium heat.
2. Cook for 6 to 8 minutes.
3. Transfer mixture to a blender.
4. Remove thyme sprigs.
5. Stir in the remaining ingredients.
6. Pulse until smooth.
7. Strain mixture and freeze for 1 hour.

Nutrition:

Calories: 78 Fat: 0 g Carbs: 20 g Protein: 3 g

Conclusion

Thank you for purchasing this book about Copycat Recipes.

Copycat Recipes are recipes that copy from famous restaurants.

This cookbook is for you to try out these recipes. This book focuses on Copycat Recipes for food. Copycat Recipes are usually easy to make. Copycat Recipes are also delicious. So, I was excited to start this book.

There are many Copycat Recipes in this book. But I selected the best ones for you to try.

I hope you will enjoy eating those foods at home!

As we end this journey, I would like to share with you some practical tips when preparing Copycat Recipes:

1. It is significant to read the recipe carefully before starting. One should read the whole recipe before starting to cook. This is very vital for the reason that everyone has diverse ways of preparing the same dish and you should understand the recipe well before starting to cook.
2. Make sure you understand the recipe
    As mentioned above, make sure you have understood the recipe well before starting to cook. One should also check for ingredients as some recipes require specific ingredients which are not widely available such as one ingredient found in a certain town or country.
3. Always use fresh ingredients, never canned, dried or frozen ones.
    We should always use fresh ingredients for our cooking. The best way to know if an ingredient is fresh is by its appearance,

texture and smell. If the recipe calls for canned, dried or frozen ingredients but fresh ones are available, the recipe should be amended to accommodate this difference because canned, dried or frozen ingredients will not produce the same results as fresh ones.

4. One should always follow the recipes exactly as written.
   This is very important because cooking recipes are carefully devised according to a certain method that will not work when it's changed.

5. Cooking and baking recipes should be done in a well-ventilated area.
   Cooking or baking is one of the basic requirements for preparing Copycat Recipes. Cooking and baking will produce a lot of steam which can be harmful if they're done in a bounded space for example a kitchen with no ventilation.

6. Always wear proper clothing when cooking or baking
   Make sure to wear proper clothing while cooking; it is not advisable to cook or bake wearing very tight clothes because this kind of clothing can get caught in moving parts like moving blades, grinding blades and other kinds of equipment used in food preparation, cooking or baking.

7. Use fire-proof tools and equipment when preparing Copycat Recipes
   When preparing Copycat Recipes, it is important to use fire-resistant tools and equipment like silicon handled cooking spoons which are very handy when deep frying or boiling oil because they can withstand high heat; also, nonstick cookware has become popular because of its ability to prevent food from sticking to them and being ruined.

8. When baking cakes, make sure you grease the pans well with butter or oil before pouring the batter in them.
   If you don't grease the pans well, it can cause your cake to stick on the pan.

9. Always test your cake for doneness by inserting a toothpick on its center. If it comes out clean, it means the cake is already made; if there's still batter in the toothpick, put the cake back to bake until no more batter sticks on the toothpick when inserted into its center.

10. When preparing Copycat Recipes always make sure that excess water has been drained before frying or cooking food items like fried chicken and French fries.
    The excess water can be drained by letting the food item sit for about 10 minutes before cooking.

11. When preparing Copycat Recipes, never leave a cooking pot unattended on the kitchen range since the sudden fire and boilovers can happen at any moment especially when deep-frying.

12. When preparing Copycat Recipes, always read the recipe first before going to the grocery store, because ingredients in some recipes are very specific and may not be available in other stores; it is important to have all the ingredients in hand before starting to cook so you will not waste your time looking for them.

13. When preparing Copycat Recipes, always use ingredients of high quality and freshness. Ingredients for Copycat Recipes should be fresh and of high quality. When a recipe calls for fresh ingredients but the ingredients we have are not, we should substitute it with another ingredient that will produce similar results. (There is an example in this book where you can do this).

14. Be certain to wash your hands earlier and afterward preparing Copycat Recipes.
    You might accidentally touch your eyes or other parts of your body during cooking which may cause infection; always wash your hands before starting to cook so you will not contaminate the food you are about to cook.

15. Before defrosting frozen ingredients, always make sure that your kitchen is well-ventilated.
Frozen foods like meats and vegetables should be thoroughly defrosted before cooking; if you try to use them while they are still frozen, they can have bad effects on your health. They can also spoil other ingredients in food.
16. When storing leftover food, always store them in air-tight containers and refrigerate immediately after storing it.
If we don't refrigerate our leftovers right away, bacteria can grow on our food and cause food poisoning.
17. Continuously wash your hands subsequently touching raw food.
When preparing Copycat Recipes, always wash your hands after touching raw ingredients like eggs and meats; bacteria from these foods can infect other ingredients in food that you are cooking.
18. Be sure to use clean utensils when preparing Copycat Recipes
When handling food to be cooked or baked, always make sure that the utensils you are using are free from any kind of impurities; if they're not, bacteria can grow on them which may contaminate the food.

Thank you again for using this book as your guide to preparing Copycat Recipes.

We hope that this book has been helpful in providing inspiration and guidance for cooking at home.

Thank you again for purchasing this book on Copycat Recipes!

Always remember that cooking is very easy if we follow the right procedures.

Enjoy the book!

Cooking Conversion Charts

COOKING CONVERSION CHART

Measurement

CUP	ONCES	MILLILITERS	TABLESPOONS
8 cup	64 oz	1895 ml	128
6 cup	48 oz	1420 ml	96
5 cup	40 oz	1180 ml	80
4 cup	32 oz	960 ml	64
2 cup	16 oz	480 ml	32
1 cup	8 oz	240 ml	16
3/4 cup	6 oz	177 ml	12
2/3 cup	5 oz	158 ml	11
1/2 cup	4 oz	118 ml	8
3/8 cup	3 oz	90 ml	6
1/3 cup	2.5 oz	79 ml	5.5
1/4 cup	2 oz	59 ml	4
1/8 cup	1 oz	30 ml	3
1/16 cup	1/2 oz	15 ml	1

Temperature

FAHRENHEIT	CELSIUS
100 °F	37 °C
150 °F	65 °C
200 °F	93 °C
250 °F	121 °C
300 °F	150 °C
325 °F	160 °C
350 °F	180 °C
375 °F	190 °C
400 °F	200 °C
425 °F	220 °C
450 °F	230 °C
500 °F	260 °C
525 °F	274 °C
550 °F	288 °C

Weight

IMPERIAL	METRIC
1/2 oz	15 g
1 oz	29 g
2 oz	57 g
3 oz	85 g
4 oz	113 g
5 oz	141 g
6 oz	170 g
8 oz	227 g
10 oz	283 g
12 oz	340 g
13 oz	369 g
14 oz	397 g
15 oz	425 g
1 lb	453 g

My Recipes

Recipe Name _____

Preparation Time:

Serving:

Difficulty Level:

Ingredients

_____
_____
_____
_____
_____
_____
_____
_____
_____

Steps for preparation

_____
_____
_____
_____
_____
_____
_____
_____
_____
_____
_____
_____
_____
_____
_____

Recipe Name _____

Preparation Time:

Serving:

Difficulty Level:

Ingredients

_____

_____

_____

_____

_____

_____

_____

_____

Steps for preparation

_____

_____

_____

_____

_____

_____

_____

_____

_____

_____

_____

_____

_____

_____

Recipe Name _____

Preparation Time:

Serving:

Difficulty Level:

Ingredients

_____
_____
_____
_____
_____
_____
_____
_____
_____

Steps for preparation

_____
_____
_____
_____
_____
_____
_____
_____
_____
_____
_____
_____
_____
_____
_____
_____

Recipe Name _____

Preparation Time:

Serving:

Difficulty Level:

Ingredients

_____
_____
_____
_____
_____
_____
_____
_____
_____

Steps for preparation

_____
_____
_____
_____
_____
_____
_____
_____
_____
_____
_____
_____
_____
_____
_____

CPSIA information can be obtained
at www.ICGtesting.com
Printed in the USA
BVHW061759230321
603262BV00006B/649